Private Collection

By Anna Cellmer

First published in April 2014 in Lulu Publisher

This is an exquisite collection of my favorite poems from previous anthologies
Hope you will enjoy this little trip through a feelings world

Have an enjoyable read

Anna Cellmer

Welcome on my pages and please contact me any time you need it ☺

annaela3@gmail.com

http://stores.lulu.com/annaela3
https://www.facebook.com/pages/Daily-Crumbs-poetry-collections-by-Anna-Cellmer/152073201656457
https://www.facebook.com/opengatesbyAnnaCellmer
https://www.facebook.com/pages/Beautiful-Stranger-by-Anna-Cellmer/211403929016220
https://www.facebook.com/soundofsilencebyannacellmer
https://www.facebook.com/anna.cellmer

The puzzle

Closed in the tin of my own
I forgot about the essence of the world
Remembered in this dance
Whirling, I come in more and more deeply
Inwards of my own images
But it's not me who is the riddle
On which all look for the answer
Nor even none of you
We are only the element of the puzzle
In order to find out
A right place in suitable time
In order to not destroy the world
In order to not overlook its chance
Of participation in evolution of the life
And then look into the eyes
With a pride - not a shame...

The kiss

I run through the rainbow
Drenching my mouth
In the pastels - tints
Of its passing,
Absorbing every touch of its colour
This warmth I love,
It pulsates in blood,
And I penetrate
Across its variety,
Pages of you
To become only
The small particle
Drinking from your mouth
My own soul

Waltz with death

I touch the interior of a black abyss
And I feel death in my hand
I turn her over in my fingers
I dance with her in the moonshine
The shameless waltz of my dark thoughts
I penetrate her incorporeality
And I feel that I have her in me
She is the miraculous well
In which I would like to sink every day
And touch her soul,
And tear to pieces her heart
To absorb all
What is concealed before me

Three nights in Zakopane

I ran to you on meeting
And I became drunk on your closeness
We plunged to each other
And we fell amazed
Lasting in this joyful intoxication
We couldn't find places
In bed our amusement
Laughing
I trembled as a leaf
In the gust which you were
With cold and fright
Before the storm which fell on me
I clung to you
How I would want to conceal myself in you
And you trembled yet more strongly
Apologizing...
You uncovered me
Now I had to find you
In darkness, blindfolded
You led me, you helped
Because alone I was yet too shy
In order to look before me
I felt guilty now
Sacrilege.

The conqueror

You entered on my territories
You mastered them without question
Like William the Conqueror
I kept silent, expressing agreement
With your English imperialism
And now what, you resign?
Then fear tells you to put out
This what you earlier lighted
You want peace suddenly
You play the diplomat
You want friendship but you forgot
But a moment ago
You already had almost all.

Mirror Room

Irreplaceable
You are reflected in everyone,
The sight, the palm,
the mouth
My Mirrored room
Everywhere you
And only you
Even in his eyes different
Even in his embraced
Tool caress
Replaced I am
Not good enough
To take your place
On the other side of the mirror
Soon I will find a stone

To break all this glass around!

Out naivety!
Out illusion!

It is me who is left
And my emptiness
I don't want anything
Your circulating husbands
Your handles and uvulas
Asking about so little
And you as well
All you are nothing but escape
I can't break anything
Because you are my reflection
All and you this exceptional one too
Without you I am like a mirror
In a room without light
In a darkness
I don't see anything there is no me
So I go out on meeting you
To see myself again
In my reflection
To not forget that I exist.

Underground

I go down underground
The hazard of existence
And I am in this tunnel
Of delightful submission
Windingly
With the laughter
I bite through fetters
Of reasonable honesty
And I drown in the puddle
Of ecstatic repugnance
Insecure tomorrow

Distance

I don't feel you so strongly now
Your smell grows flat
It stayed only
An empty gust of oblivion
Your eyes walk away
How birds flock
Disappearing in the blue of the ocean
But I stay here
Pressing in my small world
Again putting to shame
My own steps
And hands without support
I am not already strong
Loneliness wraps around me its overcoat
We become one
It is my soul
I became its incarnation
I got lost in it
I do not know where I am
I don't know who I am
It is everywhere.

Calmness

The priestess of calm normality
Lives here temporarily
She tries to cover the skies
Black chaos of the nonentities
She smiles condescendingly
Reconciled with the world
I measure her time
When she will fall out from the corner
When she will meet with an accident
And I will jump in the precipice again.

Wandering

I've got lost in this way to you
Constantly wandering aimlessly
Looking for beauty in space
But what is it for?
When I still go to you
And seeing you I go away
Because it is still too far
Even standing face to face
Distance doesn't get smaller
So I run away further
To a feeling that I lose again
Crying to miss you again
No ocean will cover me your eyes
No mountain routes will make me forget...
And however I err further
Having a hope that once
I wont need to go away

Meeting you once more

You returned in dreams again
About the blue of your eyes
So sweet...
About kisses
So delightful
And about touch
So penetrating,
So true...
How every word
Sunk in memory
Of our moments
You fed me
The sight of you
And you are in me again
How alter ego
How the answer
For all the questions
How reassuring
For uncertainty
How the source of new hope
Not ending
The history of our hearts.

Win a while

I shifted the figures
Running into you
Pawns in this game of life
We move with grace
On the chart of existence
Coming across
On the king, the proper step
The Victory
A while of authenticity
In this game of feelings
Then there is the smile of the sun
On chosen faces
Maybe fleeting
But it's worth
Every time
To win a while

Dance of love

Every little step runs out in the future
Which is nothing but a moment
We live for
So I make sure myself
That you are, that you wait
There for this time
When again you will cover my world
And I will see only
The smile of your eyes
So sweet
I wait for the darkness
From which you will go out
To take me
Inwards of your soul
I wait for the palms
That kidnap me for the fire
In which we will burn
When again it absorbs us
This dance of our hearts

First night

I gave myself up today
For you
Near you
Though it was not you near me,
I gave myself up
Giving nothing more
Except me
And you do not even know
How this a little.
I cried today
By you
Near you
Though you didn't
See my tears
I cried
Feeling nothing more
Except sorrow
That this is not you
Who lies by me.

Dedication

I'm with you
For your hands giving me delight
For life that you feed me
For memories still alive
For music, for wine
For this trip into the unknown
For you I'm
For the loneliness that I kill
For the while of happiness that I give
For laughter that I infect
For the adventure that you wanted

I'm Sarah

I am Sarah, drowsy and wet
To worship his deity
On different ways
I am woman trippant
World right next to
Leaving remembrance
I am a cloud which the wind
Propels over the ground
I am a shadow which you touch
And I disappear
Because I do not exist for you

Far from you

The trip the next day
An unnecessary trip
Which I dedicate to you
How every action
Even this the most prosaic
I look at the world
In order to know more
In order to give you
Still more
I fear only
To lose you en route
I fear
That I will not find the road
To you
Because I will go too far
Because I will crash
Skipping in to the precipice
From which
There is no return

Coming back to you

I forgot
For a moment
About your existence
Immersed in a dream
In reality
Gorged with delicacies
of the World
Passed me on tray
With a wine binding
I walked away
To stop for a moment
Think about you
And I come back now
Yours again
Washed from sin
By love
To you
Even without you
Even not with you
Always Yours

Waiting for you

I swung with branches
A tree without roots free in space
Summoning it to flight
With every day its crown grows
Liberated by the pressure
Of the corset of youth
They would rustle so loudly
Summoning its lover
Who it lives for
Who it dances for
The wild dance of nature
Among the rocky hills
Together with the wind
Playing on the waves
Melody bursts of passion
I call You
My lover
Among the night
I call You
The hum of the wind
I call You
The scream of the storm
You would crash
There on the island
Where I wait
If you want
I will be a willow
To be able to
Wreathe Your shoulders
So that You could hear
The melody of the bird's wings
Fluttering among the branches
If you want
I will be a rock
Where You will reach
Looking for refuge
After a long cruise
If I could
To take You in
Exposing all the caves
In which you could fall asleep
You could be a discoverer
You could wander
Over pulsating valleys and hills
You could conquer all the hilltops
You could find the roads to fiery cave
And I will feel Your every movement
You will touch me
With the sounds of music
Which you will feel in your heart
You will be the pianist
Which will play on me
The song awakening to the life
I call to You
My Dear
Standing on the rocks,
Gazing at the Ocean
Dressed in a gown
Of gossamer and fog
And with a necklace of morning dew
You would arrive to marry me
Because I'm Your goddess
Sailor
I call hopeful
That you will land on the island
Where I wait.

Missing you

I still look for you
I miss you all the time
Listening with attention in the silence
One's small sadness and sweet joys
I'm a reflection of the events of a day and night
To stand up again before the wall
Silent loneliness closed somewhere there, in the centre of my being
Deaf to words an insecure nobody, wanting nothing
Abstract from the world perfect and beautiful
In one's hopes on self annihilation.

To all special men I meet on my way

I like you those who I meet on my way
I like these halts a silent agreement
I like your eyes so full of understanding
So similar and speaking more than your mouth
Though they also speak this truth so well known
Because my own
Sometimes undiscovered but this way even more significant
I like you
Less than Lovers more than friends
Who know more from others
Those who never had any chance
To perceive this path
Which is possible to pass together
Even if only just to the first crossing road.

Love's prophecy

Sunken by you
Forever
I became a shell
Listening with attention, waiting,
For the high tide
You would tackle me
Inside you
Relishing
The magnitude of your love
My ocean
The most ubiquitous

Every road
Which takes me away
From you
Is incorrect
Every moment
Even the merriest
Far from you
Is lost
Because only you are
My source of love
And my happiness
The most essential

So I wait
Turning back
From the incorrect roads
Which I tread
Wanting for a moment
To get away
From your power
In vain
When the moon also
Prompts me the words
That I'm yours

How could I
Not believe it?
When even my heart
Laughs
Into this sweetest
Prophecy

How could I
Distrust my own heart
Which screams
For you, and it knows
That it is you!

Oh, my poor words!

Imprisoned in the category of the one small picture
I became the slave of affectionate sentimentality
Asking myself about the magnitude
In name of words - the pretenders of Love
O, mad words!
Desirous more than you can receive,
Do not ask about the fame
And the name of the Poetry
Of the Ages Size
Because you've been sewn
Nothing but one person measure
Looking of the second one
The small picture of lyrical magnificence
Choke further
In your longing town
Because it isn't time yet
For creation of the new dimensions
You are too young still
To such terrific transubstantiations
You are as The Little Prince
Who could stir up too much
In this world of undiscovered values
By his defiant orders
So paint yourself further
The crystal small picture
Until you will grow up to the perfection
And you will shoot
Of the thousand crystalline flowers
Which become rooted in the ground
That the sons and daughters would be born
The Masters and Margaritas
Gods and constructors
The new order of the world.

The sparkling herds
The imps of Idleness
Pierce me thoroughly
That they would extricate oneself
The pearly Mass
Of Impertinent Blaze
The uncontrollable Joy

O, my poor words!
You felt ashamed because you don't know
Whether you have something to say – to this world
You got scared
This tale about yourself
But this it is not a crime
You can play with yourself
To arrange in the sky constellations
To get to the core of the essence of life
And to die, uncovering nothing new
You can play in the gravediggers
Or the scatterers more
Nobody keeps you under command
Because it is me who keeps the reins
Of this Carriage of Words
And I love this rough ride and laugh
Of my own words
Speeding up to the unconsciousness
How the fiery Arabs
On the new road
To obscene and disobedient
Unknowing

So drive further!
My pearly steeds
To the unknown distinction
To the open sensuality
To the beginning of endlessly
Or with the many ends
To a peak of iceberg
Inside of impenetrable nothingness
Wherever
You can take me
Where I will die
Whipped and whipping
The Whip of contempt and the revolt
Against Everything
That dares my attention
That I'm going too fast
Or maybe in the wrong direction.

Oh, fool unbelievers
Of Existence the open border with the miracle!
How come you arrest me on the road
How come you don't believe in my Words?
Rushed on the cards
To the Meeting of the Perfect Truth?

I laugh to you with the words
Which are playing with themselves
Stimulating my soul
To the Orgasm of Survival
And what else I can expect
From these words which don't care about the fame?

Lost lover

You got lost my dream lover
Your ship sank in the depths of life
Among which you forgot where you have to swim
You crashed on the rocks
Which I poured out from the last tears I shed for you
I am free now in the isolation of this place
Expectant of betrothed
I go there now where he waits
This one who is and will be
And to whom I'm whispering
And he is so close that I hear his voice
Even when he keeps silent,
The one who I feel
The one who I see
The one who is me
Because I am his

Travelling thoughts

November nights of great cities
Where the hotel - love dies
Torn with the anchor of life
With the scream spitting out the world
Again, with the future
I rummage the time in rubbish bins
To find the essence of the rights
Ruling over immortality

Dipped in the twilight of space
Swing with hips to raise the laughter
Which overfills me through and through
To shout no existing names
To express a charm tells
Which are thundering sluggishly
Through the waves
Caressing my soul
By unremembered songs of the world.

The gentle space raises my body
To pour on himself with the surface
Seeking of the liberation
Somewhere behind the horizon
Of the Uncertainty
The Life depends of the power of shoulders
Groping for
the Resting-place
Would be possible to come back home
And at this time?

The shadow

I find myself in the shadow as a stranger
Who takes a part in this life by accident
Almost as an intruder
Who doesn't know the rules of this game
I try to put on a brave face
This that within me I do not really care
Of the things so close to me
The deepest love we feel is this far away
This that we can't touch looking far on the horizon
That we reach on the stars
But not this one which is so close
To become everyday life so simple as the baby's cry
Demanding to change its nappy
But I'm coming back to you
Seeing you covering boys while you look at them
With such tenderness that tears put away
This internal voice which is pushing me
To the circle of magical dreams
That are stifling this love with the smell of life

Little days

I live the natural rhythm of everyday life
To step by days in a year
The saint deliberation without
Angry for all these little events around
Which are creating my reality right now
Without inspiration of not realized teenager anymore
The wild chariots of passion are gone
And I'm mixed with some comical little things
I take this rule seriously that is imposed to me by life
Not sure of aims I should go for
Not sure of methods I use every day
Sure only you
That you forgive me
Every uncertainty I have within.

After years....

Secret

I gushed betraying my secret
Stored already
In the secret chest of my being
God's whether you know how does happiness look?
Because I know I am happiness
My heart sings the sun lit me again
I love, I love,
I love!
And only this matters
And you know this.

Silence

You keep silent
You don't know again
What to do
With this love
It crushed you
So suddenly
That you gnaw on your thoughts
What to answer
On such a call?
And now
Maybe you've already forgot
Where this path leads
Where you never went
Lover
My cold English Man
Don't be so cold for me
Just let me love you
Or let me go
Because you are my desire
Until I will be sure
That you are dead to me
I just need to know
What your heart
Is telling you
About me.

Melody

No one feels the same melody in his heart as I do
Even you, all you are just an imagination
No one can feel the same
Orient express with dance as I do
No one can give me this orgasm that I need
Even you can't I'm alone again
On this simple world with its roles without any sense
Just simple giving and simple taking
Little, little things to do to make each other comfortable
I can't stand that situation
I want here the life comes true
My Truth with all meanings
In your tongue in your lips
In your hands and voice
And the music in my heart
I need that.

Visit

Are you single?
I am asking because...
I'd like to visit you
Someday
Some night
I'd like you to wait
For me
Alone
That's why I ask
I just need to come
To you
But I don't know
Your address
Is it a problem for you
That I'm going
To visit you
Without my clothes?

Queen of this game

I change my name
Almost every day
Once I start to be brave
And I see myself
So strong, so great
As a queen of this game
As a woman from your dream
As the Athena with
The sword of words
To win this premier price
You, I mean
But you know
That sometimes I'm so weak
And I can't even speak
Standing so close to you
And I don't know at all
What to do with this heart
So broken-down, so afraid of
This real truth or of even you
And this life too
Please help me
To understand
What should I do
To be with you
My friend.

Dream

I want a big house
I want to listen the music around
I want to play with my thoughts
I want to dance
I want to wait
For you inside
I want to see the ocean down
I want to take a bath
Naked delighting in the waves
Which are caressing me in the sun-rising light
And I want to come back
To our great bed
When you are just waking up
My Man
I love you then
And you are
With me again

I wish to know your habits

I wish to know
Your daily habits
You live alone, so
You must like something
And dislike too
I wish to know
All of these
Little things
You do
I wish to be
Someone who can
Understand the man
As you are, my friend
I wish to know
Your thoughts
And desires
And your silence
I think I can
Forgive you
Everything you could do
And I wish to know
How it is with you

Invitation

Come inside me
I want this so hard, Darling
Please come inside

Could you touch me there?

Could you touch me
There?
And here...
And here...
And here yet ..Oh yes
And don't forget
About this...
And there...
And here...
And here yet...
Oh it's wonderful
And here...
Here... Yes
A little more yet
Please
And here...
There..Yes
And there...
And here...
Here...
Oh, don't forget
About my little finger yet
Oh, my Sweet Boy
You are just wonderful tonight
Let me touch you now...
Let me kiss...
Yes I wish...

Desert

desert
time is going
quickly
slowly
some things to do
to control
make a coffee
dinner, TV
suddenly
something happened
excitement
talk hot
high feel
strange smile
the end
desert
little things
around
dreams
life hope
for the next
feelings wave
in the air.

Cold inside

When I'm not in love
I feel this special sadness
Inside
When I start again
To be with the man
But I need to be a woman
So I go to another
Who makes me feel this way
And for a while it's OK
But this sadness inside
Is still racking my heart
To the end
Of the new romance
With the man
I'm not in love
I can't love anymore
If I know
That the man
I wish to be with
Is so close but silent
And
In the deep of my heart
I'm still with him
In my dream
Lying with husband
Trying to love a new one too
Always this same
Sadness of the heart
After another cold night
Cold inside.

Wicked game

You said that I don't hurt you
This way
You don't love me then...
So, it's just a wicked game
Between the woman
And the man who understand
And you know
I'm not sure if it's sad at all
It's just a different kind of me
Which likes this play
With you and me and this cold love
In the hotel room
Where I know
I can do whatever I want
And you too
Because it's just a play
Between the woman and the man
Who understand

Life

Life is just a collection
Of the different
Impressions which exists
During a day
Inside us and around
This place we live in
It's kind of mish-mash
Of our feelings
Thoughts and this is
What really happens
To us
During these lessons
We get all the time
In our life.

Be a realist

I hate this word
I hate and why I must to hear this so many times
"Be a realist" I hate to be a realist
Why should I like this, why?
I hate to be just a good wife
I hate to live in my town all my life I need to fly
I hate this science carrier too
I want to be an artist, a poet, a writer, a dancer too
Whatever it's not important at all
I want to be a woman in love
But I don't need to be a realist no, no, no!
I hate this kind of job being a realist means to me
Just to live normally but it is so boring and mean
It's like nothing just things without any meaning
I never want to be the realist no and I wish to find someone
Who let me not to be a realist
Who let me fly, who let me sing
I need the love to dream about
I need the touch, so shy
I need the whole world in my hand
I want a real love to start again
And new dreams about the perfect man
Who is touching me by his soul
So wild, so proud, so deep and so warm
By his merrily flowing thoughts and palms
I wish to be real but not a realist at all.
Every age, every time is great
To feel so good, to feel OK
With this sensual dance
Living in an imaginary embrace
Of my thoughts, so hungry
This voice, this touch, this caress this deep ocean of desires
Hidden somewhere in the cave of their eyes
And within mine and your soul, still so mysterious, so unknown.

Just a drop

I thought I'm talking to my friend
But it seems that
You were always just a stranger
It is sad but I understand
The time is important to you
And these few days
So long ago
Do not exist anymore
Means nothing to you
Because it's just
A drop in the sea
Of this life
You used to live
Without me.

Another touch

You can be very brave to the man
You know well or long but
With another one you are
Again so shy as a teenager
It's strange feeling
It's like a new beginning
You are again as a virgin
Another time you try
But you're afraid
You don't know anything
The new start
New life
And you
Too
Is
it
not
wonderful?

Just another touch

Seeing you from time to time
I always smile inside
We speak about nothing
It's like a prelude
To something else
Something more
I don't know yet
But I like this
Somehow and I know
You like this too
So we are waiting
For another time
Another way
To find each other
Someday
Perhaps
Only in our dreams life
But it is so nice
So strange
When I see you
Again and again
It's like a ray of new day
Inside my heart
Another reason to smile
Another touch.

The doors

I let you go away to let you come along
I let you kill yourself to be alone
I'm going through my sins so proud
Being the owner of my soul
And then I want to know
Are you still there behind my door?
And then I wish to believe
That you are there still
But I'm afraid that You do not exist

Strangers

Write me another piece like this
And you will stay the lover from my dreams
Stranger
Lord, how come you let me fall in love
With another one nice man who just came and knocked to my door again
Strangers come and go
This is the way they become the part of the story
Some of them are with me, some of them are gone
This is the way the life goes on

Go one deeper

If you are not going to fall in love with me
Then go away from my dreams!
Do you want me?
I don't think so this what you want is just a little dream
But you don't want me in real
You don't expect anything, so
You have what you want this short and flat bly bly
Between the strangers we are busy man, busy man
You don't have the time for love then
But do you know what the time is for?
You are so busy as you want as you need and wish mostly
Are you the owner of your time?
Are you the master of your life?
Are you ready to go outside?
Are you able to drown within someone?

Expectations

I don't expect
You'd marry me
No, my boy
This what I want
Is something much more
I'm going to make you
The slave of love

All the truth

What the truth are you looking for
Just take me and you will see it
Within my eyes, baby
All the truth is this what turns you on
What makes you feel
This way as you feel right now
So happy with me somehow
So come on stop these silly talks
About the philosophical aspects of the world
About this special place which not exists at all
Don't say that you look for the challenge in me like this
Just come and take me in your words, in your thoughts, in real
The way is the best for you and me occasionally or still,
No matter how you wish and dream
What kind of truth do you want to know more?
Just come and take me, honey
You've won me already with this big lottery of thoughts
So you can have this what you want
You were brave enough
To stay my love

On the way

You live inside
This dream which
I used to call
My life
We never know
Where this path
Leads us
And this is
The most exciting
Part of the story

Internal words

Sometimes I try to be hard
and not write for a while to you
To make you feel this way as you do
unsure
For a while
Is this love real
Are you in love with me still?
But my words are growing in me
And then I just can't
To not let you know
That I care that I want
you
I wont beg you for anything
I'm strong enough to not do it
But I miss your words
The sight of you
Momentarily I'm scared
That you go away but I know
That everything will be ok
I still have hope
For this special love
But if you ever decide to
Not start this in real
Please tell me
Tell me everything you think
I'm so hungry your soul
Within me
If you decide to go away
I'll understand
I'll be sad
But life is like that
And we both must want
This same
To make this love
Great
Every day with you inside
Is like a new way
new beginning, another start

We can say hello
and we can say goodbye
I have had this dark thoughts
From time to time
That you don't care
That you would stop it and go away

But then
I can't, I can't stop my self
I wish to have you
Someway
Even with your stillness
And when you are so silent
Even if you don't come to me
And if I wont come to you
I still want to be with you
And I can't play with you
In silence game
To let you
Be hungry me
more
I'm not able to do that yet
So forgive me
That I let you know again
That I'm with you
That you are my man

I love to know this

How I love to know
That you are my man
That you are my love
How I love to see
The words of you so sweet
To me
How I love to wait
When I know that you will come
Soon
To give me so much pleasure
To give me so much joy
How I love to be yours
How I love to believe
That you will come to me
For real

Sorrow

Sometimes I think
That if I'd reach
Only for you
To come to me
I'd probably die
From sorrow
That you don't come
That all I see
Is just an empty space
Where you should be
So I have to
Keep whole the world
During this time
When you have been gone
When I'm waiting for you
Alone

Come tonight

Yes you're right, my love
We don't need to hurry up at all
We have a lot of time
To meet each other
Step by step
We will know more and more
That you would fill my soul
To complete me whole
I don't want to disappoint you
Not at all
I just love to hear your voice
I just need to be sure of it
That you feel the same
What I feel
That's why I write
All these things
But I believe
That you want me still
And I have hope
For this love
That wont disappoint
Anyone
I'm so hungry of your words
I'm curious of your soul
Your point of view
For the things
Your relationships
Your life which you live
As much as your touch and kiss
As much as your palms and lips on me

I want you whole in me
Please complete me
Be within
This is my dream
But you know
That I wish still
To have your heart
So I will try
To be this right girl
If you wish
Even living here
Within your dreams
About me
I wish to make you happy
And I know you want this same
And I love this
I want this
I need
So, please come to me
When I'll go to sleep
Come to my dream
I need to feel your touch inside
I wish to hold your mind
And kiss you for good night
Tonight

Forgive me

You are silent
It always makes me a bit sad
Especially when before that
I had written something what
I regret
When I'm too emotional
To you sometimes,
When I have my black thoughts
or doubts,
And I have put them all to you
Then this silence,
Then I feel
Such an emptiness
Such a idle day,
You blend into me as a tree
I'm not sure how I could live
Without you
I don't want even to imagine this
You are within me
And it's enough to live
And to feel
Everything
That is possible
And to love you still
Forever and ever I will

And forgive me
Every doubt
I have had so far
Every bad word
Every thought
Which is against
Our love,
You and me,
Which is because
I feel so weak
Sometimes
Without your arms
Around me

Missing your thoughts

The whisper of love
Came to my soul again
But I'm not sure of your heart
Still
As I know you
And this
What do you want
The most
My Dear
Perhaps you don't have
Whole my heart yet
But it doesn't mean
That you can't take me tonight
I'm suspicious still
A bit
But it doesn't mean
That I don't love you
Because I do
Yes I do
It's just that
I'm still unsure
This what you hide inside
I'm still afraid that
You and I it's just a dream
Which can't exist in reality
By the way
You make my days so full of life
You make my heart so full of smiles
I'm so glad to find you
but
How I wish to be sure
That we can survive the time
All this time
When we are not together,
Do you think of me still
Even when I'm silent
Even when you are silent,

When we don't see
We don't touch each other
When we don't see our thoughts,
When we do so many things around
And we don't know anything about this?
I need your words as an air
Please come and say
That you love me
And you care
I don't like it that
When I'm silent
You are like this too
At this time I'm afraid
Our love is not growing
At all
At this time
We can stay strangers again
You and I can disappear
I don't want this
I feel good with you
I feel as a part of your life
As a part of you
But these whiles
When I'm not sure
Annoying me a bit
But I can't do anything
Where are you?
My love?
And why so little time
You can spend with me,
Why you don't want
To share your soul freely
You don't need
You don't feel you have to, perhaps
But I miss your words
I try to live normally
And enjoy other things
But I miss your thoughts
And I'm afraid of this love
I don't want to lose
Something so special, so good
I get from life again,
So please don't let me think
This way
Come and say
That you live, that you think
And you are with me still
In this dream

You who stayed

I place my thoughts
Before the sight of you
Searching this longing
I have still inside
Looking for the man
As you are
I find my self
In an empty space
Of wanting
Lost in the world
Which is just a flash
Of touching words
Floating from your minds
Across the light of my screen
The window is open wide
For all of these rays of smiles
Curiosity is a guider of mine
So I'm still looking around
To another one small world of your own
To catch to feel to feed my soul
But only you is this one
Who stayed for good
To belong
To want
To love
To waiting for

Your new girl

You don't even know how it hurts
such words, but don't worry about
It's just because I love you
I think I'll be fine soon, I hope
It's just for a while I feel so bad
Like all the world just become gray
from now
when I see that you are not mine
that you just found another one
girlfriend to love
but thank you
that you are so honest with me
my love
I was afraid that this dream is too good
and that someday
something will happen like this
something wont be just as i wish
but i know that it's not possible
to live just like this with me
I know I understand
your need to be with some real warm girl
by your side
but today you just realized me again
who I'm
I'm just married and mother
living so far away from you
I can't give you this what she can do, I'm sure
So maybe I should just go away with all this love
to leave you in peace with another one
I just feel so sad now but I understand
I wish you the best
I hope you are ok
If you ever need me
Let me know
I'm still here for you
But I think that I should
Just leave you alone right now
I think I should leave you
yes I think
Yes I'll try I promise
I'll try to not be sad
because of this fact
that my perfect man
have a new girlfriend
from now
yes I'll try to survive
but how to believe in your words of love
how to understand clear
I'll try to live with this somehow
but I wont fight
I don't have the chance
to win with the reality
but come back to me

when you will need me
come back when you will be free
and for me
goodbye for now
my sweet man
goodbye
don't think about me too much
it wont be good for your new girlfriend
for this new relationship which you start to build
try to be happy with her
just remember
That I'm where I'm
Just enjoy your new love
forget about me
God how I'm sad telling this
A pity girl
but maybe tomorrow I'll be fine
and I'll understand better
and I'll try to smile
but for now
I can't I'm sorry I can't
It was just too beautiful
that It could be real
but you know that I wish you the best on your way
don't forget me
don't forget
I know it was hard to you
to live with this love alone
but now
it's so hard to me
To live with this fact
that you have a new one
but I'll try
Yes I'll try
Just can't stop these tears fall down
right now

Where is your heart now?

I love you,
Yes you are right
Nothing has changed between us darling,
I've had just this sad night
Because of this what you said to me recently
It's hard to me sometimes
To find out again this reality around,
Yes you need someone by your side,
Maybe I don't like my life at all
But I don't know how could i change this now
I lived in this dream about perfect love
And now I have to wake up for a while
Everything is good if we feel both good with this so
I'll try to accept you new life and love now

oh
But it was just a week ago
When you said
That you are mine
That you love me
And that I should remember this
Always
How it is now
My sweet
How it is
Where is your heart
Placed
Where it is?
Tell me please

Agreement

You just killed one dream
That I'd leave for you
my home
but I still can find another one
dream to live by
you just turn this love
into simple affair
but it's OK
I can live with this
I suppose
maybe it's even better dream
for both
yes my love

Life and poetry

poetry
warped scraps of reality
raised on summits of thoughts
dressed into forms perfect less or more
to amuse, to believe, to feel, to penetrate furtively
into this what we call an existence
life
Is just this what flows
among one and the second line

You miss me

I love to feel you
This way
As I do today
After your words
Always so sweet to me
I love to hear
Your voice
I love to know
That you miss me
Darling
I love you
Still and
I want you
More and more
Every day
And I'm glad
To come back
To you
With whole my body and soul
I love to be yours
As you know
Never forget about this
My love
You miss me
That's all I need
To feel you
Inside me

It's for you right now

You say you love my poetry
You say you read it
you eat it, you drink
Maybe it's just because
I put my heart
To every word I write
And you know too
That most of it is for you
I came to this world
To make you happy, you know
To make you my man, my friend
and my lord
So, enjoy

You get on me baby

Such a simple word
"I miss you"
But how much to enjoy
I feel this so merrily within
It's such a pick to my soul
Such little word
Which makes me yours
I can't run away
From you, my love
One your word
And I'm back
To you
From my tour
Not important how far
I was for a while
From you
But always in sight
Of your heart
I'm yours
So happily yours
Whole my body
Is so soft for you
Just wanting
To be touched
How you make me feel this way
My boy
How you are doing this
I don't know
But I love
And I'm so glad
That you come.

Love words

You have my artistic passion
And you have my love
What do you need more?
"Your body"
Then come
"I'm coming to you"
Oh, god
My body
You want
How I'm happy
To hear your words
You always know so well
What to answer
Of my questions
Lover

You talk to me
As I want
That's why
I love you
As no one before

How I'm glad
You want
My body more
Than my love
and art

That's what
I wanted to know
To love you more
This night
It's so easy to become
Impatient again
From two days
I'm thinking
About you here
Because of your words
So sweet
„I'm coming to you"

And now I'm not sure
Are you coming just right now?
Or in the future we will have
Someday
And again
I'm so hungry you
Your eyes
Your hands
Your lips on me
And you within
I've found some new possibility for us
Some place unknown
But I do not want
To interrupt
In your life
I've learnt to wait
For you
I do not want
To interrupt
In this dream
I enjoy
Just my thoughts
About you
I don't need to talk
I don't need to call
To tell you this
But I still wish
To share with you
Some of these thoughts
Like before and I love to wait

For the signs
From your side
I love
When you are coming
To my world
So suddenly
I love my reactions
Of this
It's amazing for me still
Discovering this love
Inside my body and soul
It is wonderful

Don't worry about me

You turned your back on the crowd
But remember
That here is the heart
Which is beating for you
So never mind
And come back to me soon
I'll be waiting for you
Whole my life through
I'm not impatient now
You know that
You have my heart
So you can go away
For as long as you need
As long it is necessary,
Don't worry about me
I know how to feed my soul
By smiles beauty and love

Lovely words

Sexy message
I received
From you today
So do it all
It wont be difficult
To you
I suppose
I love your words
You make me
Wanting you
So easily
So softly
And so good
You are doing this every time
You come here
My love
Except these whiles
When you
Are just leaving me
Or when you talk about
Another girl
You were busy with
Recently
But if you only come here
To make me yours
I'll be screaming for more
I'm sure of this
My boy
You are still the best
Lover I have
So come just
And take and do
What you are talking about
From some time

Sweet sexy words

Sweet sexy words
I hear
From your mouth
And it makes me feel
So wonderful
So happy
And so wanting you
My boy
Every little word
Of yours
Is like a prayer
Is like a song
To my soul
I can feed my self like this
And live
And believe
And dream
About this holy night
Which will come
Soon
In the shadow
Of another day
Which just flowed away
With joy
That you share with me
This special dream
And that we live
So beautifully
We are the lucky ones aren't we?
We have everything
Love, desire and this special joy
Which the woman can give the man
Which the man can give the woman
In love.

You are this one

I love you
"And I do
You are my darling"
So simple loving words between us
Which only we can feel so much
How I love to receive all these lovely answers
Of yours
You are my soul mate
You are my sweet man
I wish to be so close to you
I love to know that I'm yours
I feel you near me
And I'm not afraid
To tell you anything
And I know
You'd understand me well
And I'm sure
Your words are true
You read my soul
And you perfectly know
What I want
You are this one
I was looking for
So long.

Normal day

And another date of your coming here
Just flowed away
Did I believe this time?
Yes a bit
I put some skirt
And stockings
On me
And I was thinking
What I'd do if you call
Suddenly
And I smiled
But in the deep of my heart
I knew
That you wont come
This time
So I didn't change any plans
I have had
It was just normal day
As every other
But I still believe
That you are
With me
As always

Your eyes are sad today

Your eyes seem so sad today
What do you feel, are you ok?
Is this that you are embarrassed still
You cant speak with me or it's something more?
Maybe I have hurt you by last letters, I know
You didn't expect such news
But I cant hide anything I live by
Other way it seems no sense
To be with you if you couldn't accept
All thoughts I run for
But what is in your mind now?
What is the new dream you are looking for?
Can't I share it with you anymore?
Is it something wrong between you and me?
What does your silence mean?
I don't want to guess, my love
I prefer to believe that this what was before
Is still here living inside
To burn again someday
In the right time
In the right day
Just to see your eyes in smiles
Again.

I'm beside you still

You may not feel my touch
Laying in your bed at night
After your always busy day
When you are tired
You may not see me
Watching your sleepy eyes
Just beneath your losing dream
When you are waking up
You may not share with me
Some of your daily things
You simply live by
During your cheerful life
But remember
That no matter what you do
And if things are going
Up or down
You can be sure
That I'm here
For you
My heart never lies to me
So you know
That I'm always beside you
And I feel with this so good
That nothing can change
This simple truth

That I belong to you
And that there is nothing
More precious on this world
To me
Than our story of love
And our dream we drowned both
And you with me somehow
Together
In our dream world finding trip
Forever
So, you know me now
And I'm so bared beside you
Even living so far still
Yet close enough
To feel your breath inside me

I can't live without you

I don't like your silence
you know
and I don't feel so comfortable
anymore
but maybe you have some reason
to be like this,
there is not any problem for me
that we can't meet
I know as well as you
that it can be difficult
but I love you
and my life really started
from the time you came but
if you don't feel good with me
anymore
you can go
away
Oh no please stay
Forget it what I just said
Never go away
Please stay
I need you so much
To live
You are this one for me
Who I can trust and love
and understand
and be real with
Please don't go
How I love you
How I love
Every single inch of you
Your every thought
You are my love
You are the part of me
Don't forget it

You understand me well
You can accept me as I'm
Even this what you said at the start
About all these mythologies around
You don't believe in
Makes me sure
That we are both as one
You can play and live as me
You can understand everything
All I want to do
Is just to dance with you
So, please stay
And come to me someday
I want this so much
I can't imagine my life without
You
Here inside my heart and soul
Here within all dreams I have
Because of you

Even if for a while

If I wish to be sure something on this world
It's you my love,
but you know too that
even if you don't have too much to offer to me
it's allright too,
it's enough to believe
it's enough just to live by this
so long as it is possible,
if I say be real with me
it is just that I wish you here
to be with me so open
and familiar and just as you are
I wish to believe in your heart
and your words
always so sweet to me
but you know there wont be any consequences
if you don't,
even if it's all nothing but dream
I still appreciate that you came
to me just to light my life
even if for a while

Some moment in life

The only moment
that is really sweet
and worth to live
is this
when you say
I'm so special,
beautiful, unique
and that you need me,
want me, love me
and I believe
that it's true
This is the moment
I wish to live forever
When I'm smiling to you
swimming merrily in this charm
which you let me drown in
because life is just as you see your self
and someone else too
some little game you came
to enjoy

You just fit to me

You are not too bad
and not too good
You just perfectly fit to my soul
And you make me feel the way I love
That's all what I need to be sure
That you and me is exactly this
What I want

It's so easy now

How it is easy now
To sing my ancient whipping song of love
When you are waiting for me on the other side of this dream
With open arms
No real longings I feel inside my heart
Either wanting to be loved
If I feel and I believe in us
Someday together
So close
My love how I'm glad that you came to my heart
To live here inside

So little you

There is so little you in my life still
How can I be sure that you are real?
How to believe in this love here?
I don't know my sweet man but what can I do
I still wish that all you said to me is true
I still find the light in this way
And this what I love to believe
Is this little dream we have here
That you and me is all
What we really need
Am I wrong?
Tell me

You and me

May it be just imagination
You and me?
May it be all just mind creation
Loving here?
We never touch, we never see
So how it can be
To feel you so much
In me
Why can't I stop to think of you
My love?
Why all my life
Is running around you
Right now
Even if you seems to
Walk away into the silence
If all you said was just to please me
If all you said was nothing
You really meant
So why, why
I miss your words and you
Right now
I can fill my life by thousand
Beautiful romances
But no one can take your place
No one can create this story
Of you and me
Don't you know this?
Don't you believe
That you and me
Is something different
That you and me
Is this dream I wish to live
Forever in
That you and me
Is all I want to believe in

Let me dream then...

If love is nothing but illusion of the heart
so let me live in this dream forever
let me believe still
that you and me
is we
Don't wake me up
I love to dream like that
Don't wake me up
I want to sing my song
Till the end of love

Just came to say that you are beautiful

I can't say yet if I want anything from you
I came here just to say
That you are beautiful
And that I enjoy this that I found in your world
It's so different from this one I know
Maybe that's why it's so interesting to me
But there is something more in it
I think you are special
You gave me new smiles
You gave me wild dreams
During last night because I saw all of you
And I wished to be there too
This image so inspiring as a frightener
But beautiful and sweet the same
What to do if I see only a beauty in you
Maybe we all miss for pain as for love
Maybe we all search for this that we can't find
In this simple world?
Without going a little bit the frames out
We can't really know who we are
I found your world tender, sensual and beautiful
No real brutality is in you even when you give pain is just to feel more
Besides I always believed in the charm of new experiences
As I saw on your site how enjoyable!
Thank you, one more time to leave me with smile!
And quite excited!
That what it's all about !

Bondage

The more you bound my body the more you relieve my soul
every day I feel better with this
no chains, no fear
lives here
just love
and
the wish to give you more

This moment of light

It's such a sweet taste
Of this fresh unexpected feeling of light
That comes suddenly to you
From the sight of a beautiful stranger
Who touches your heart so merrily from the start
By look, by smile, by touch or some words
That flow gently to your soul and you know
It's something in the air again
It could be this man this special one for you
And you smile you don't know why
Just somehow
And mostly this is all you have
Just this moment in space to catch
To enjoy and to feel this something special in the air
This gentle breeze of life this little light
It can turn into many forms
Dance poetry or song
Sometimes it's a beginning of a relationship too
Sometimes even something more
You wish to believe that - in love
But only time will show this
If you want to know
Now the only thing you have is this smile
And some little need to do something more
And to go for it deeper a bit
We never know but this smile is all
We are looking for
And what we adore each time it comes to us
For good or for a while

Playing

I'm as a child
Who is playing in this
Game of life
With a smile
Sometimes I cry too
When I lose
Something I love so much
But after a while
I smile again
When I see you came
To me
again
My gentle man

It's not sex what is all about

In this what we do
It's not really sex that it's all about
Sometimes it's love yes
This something special in the air that let you sing all day
But mostly it's relationship we learn to build
To know each other more to go on our journey through the world
To know ourselves and to share smiles and joy
That's all we are for
Sex is good for a while
To know if we can go further a bit or if it is exciting
If we can create some pleasure
And dream, some trust between
And to go on without any fear into this lovely trip
Between you and me
That's all we long for

How many lovers from the dream can you handle?
Who knows this? I don't, I search
Even if I know I love this hunger to know more
Put me into another dream to live in
It's kind of madness maybe but who cares about this?
If it brings nothing but smiles and tears
If it lets me see more clear what this life is
Where is the end?
If I go to you and stay for good
Will I close all other doors?
Or I'll cherish my dreams still?
Who knows what the future brings?
Is any winner in this story of life?
Is any up and down in it?
You know that I love you
But I know also this, that love
Is the shortest from never ending things
This passion between you and me
Is all that we can really win
Let's go for it and don't think of the rest of the world
Don't care about any form just drink it
Until all is alive and full still
I know what the art is
So don't say you will teach me this
I know this life a bit or I can imagine and dream it
I need my freedom to live and to be back to you
To be sure you are this man I long for
You are the man I wish to own and kiss
To be with
I'm just not sure if this life
Is not too short or not too long
For only one story of love

The theatre

Love turned into the form of art
This site is my private theatre
And my heart plays on this scene another act
It's real though it's still the play
But love you see is here
I wish you are the main watcher and actor as well
But I don't mind to be seen by all
When I sing my song filling the pages of my life's book
I never know who will come on the stage
To let me scream or dance more
Meantime there is a peace or little monologue
But this theater still lives here and welcomes all.

Yes I know we said good bye to each other but

Yes we said goodbye
Yes I know
I'm impossible
Yes I know
I wrote too much
Yes I know I touched you
Not even once
Yes I know
That all I do is the cause of mess
Between me and you
But baby
I don't wanna lose you
If you love me still please
Don't go
Stay
Inside my world
Be here still
You know we can live
Just like this
I understand the troubles with moving
To me or to you
But all I feel is just an emptiness now
When I think you have gone
If you really have to go it's ok
But don't do it only because I did this or that
It doesn't matter at all
I love you
You should know
If it was only because some of my words
Please come back
I love you and I care
I never want to hurt you again
I never want to let you feel blue
I promise to be good.
Don't go please stay
I need you more than air

You back my love

Love is the way
You and me
Feel each other here
Love is touch
Of your words
So sweet for me
Love is faith
In you and me
Let's be together like this
My love be here for me
As I'll be
And smile to me
That's all I need
My sweet
That's all I need

Little fears of the heart

Suddenly such sadness
Flowed in to my heart
You seem to be so far away
My love my beautiful man
And I'm in the middle of this colorful crowd
Just to feel how empty is my heart right now
When I'm not sure if all I do is not
Just one step to lose you on my route
I love you
Please don't forget
I love you
And I'm just lost
Because I simply don't know what to do
To have you a bit closer to me right now
Why I must miss you so much?
Why do I waste so much time for
All around?
I'm just lost without you
And I can't stand this silence
I need breathe by love, I need
To prove my self every day
That you are this man
You are this one
I'll never ever wish to lose
I'll never ever stop to love
Even if it hurts me sometimes
When I'm not sure
If it's not too much for you
This me all
I'm so afraid you just want to go
Because you can't see here beauty
Or because it's tiring this love
Or because you don't believe anymore

Just one your word is enough

Just one your word, my love and all sadness disappeared
You are the most wonderful man of this world
And I'm the most happy and lucky girl
To have your heart and soul
I know

It's just

It's just that you fill my days by something
I can't live without any more
The most important little thing
that let all system in my mind and soul work
Without this I can't handle my days
I can't feel safe
I can't enjoy all what this life brings to me
and feel happy and feel free
to go one this journey and to love
Maybe it's because...
when you once taste
this special charm of real love
anything else is not so good for you anymore
to enjoy and to go for
Maybe I could find
a bit similar atmosphere
to create this special warm in my heart,
this belief, this charm but no it's never the same
I've found you and from now
it's just so important to me
that without it
I don't feel me enough to ever move out
to live without you inside,
so I will
But oh how happy I'm to see you again so close to me
My dear, my sweet, wonderful one
Oh yes also bad sometimes but so full of charm
In each thing you say, or you do,
you are just so beautiful
Such magic I can't resist at all
So there is no more to do but enjoy and take it all
I live by this what you offer to me
To create more love, to make you warm enough
And to make you as happy as I'm right now
With you, my love

Winter time

The winter time is coming soon between me and you
Now all we know is that you are not going to come at all
So now it's a silence time
To forget the sadness that came suddenly
To smile again one day
Perhaps to believe from the start like nothing happened
Like you really wish to come here
Like you really love and wish to be still
And for good forever mine
It's such a sweet dream we have
So it's not easy to leave it and go
To all these real things around
That are and will be still for real
But you and me have to be silent now
To forget again this little disappointment
This little shame that here is just a play
But no one should know this
Yes we have to believe still
To have this my dear
It's such a lovely thing
So special dream

What should I do?

Your love is
Just an answer of my needs
You are coming each time
I'm calling you and I wish
You to be here
When I crave for you
Using the right words
But you are never here
When I'm silent
When I'm like this
You simply disappear
How it can be?
What should I do to make you
More active, more real?

The puppet

Yes that's it
You are here
When I set the strings in motion
When I'm not doing it
You simply disappear
You exist on my request
In the world of my dreams
You are here
When I give you the sign
When I make you alive
By writing this story on and on
I need to write
To have you inside and to live
In my own theatre
In my own beautiful dream
Which became the part
Of mine and yours existence
As more I'm afraid you could disappear
As more deeply you can live here
What if I close this book?
Will you go away
Without any word?

Yes I love you still

After a few days of my silence
You doubt and ask me if I love you still?
My darling
You don't know how much it cost to be quiet to you
For a while
You don't know why?
I did this little break?
I just wished to give you a little time
To miss me
As you do right now
I was just afraid for a moment too
That you don't need me so much
As I need you
That's what this little silence was for
But you know
How much I miss you here
How much I need to be sure
Of your heart all the time
To live, to go on this beautiful life's trip
Yes I love you my darling still
And I'm so happy you miss me a bit

Just keep the touch

I wish to be close enough to hear your thoughts
But you are far now and a bit silent sometimes
I can't feel you inside
This makes me lost and I need to call
I need to ask for this little you
Inside my soul
I need your thoughts so much
Please keep the touch and love, yes love me
This is all I need to live, to smile
when I open my eyes
Waking up to another day with you here
I live to be yours don't you know?
I live waiting for another touch
From you as it was before.

Little marks

Soon the last mark on my skin
Will disappear
It will be hard to believe
All it was real
Perhaps it was just a sweet dream
We both have had suddenly
Perhaps it wasn't your lips
Touching me
Not your palms not your ...
Are you real, are you real and mine?
Or I was dreaming?
Should I forget all this here?
Do you want me to stay silent
And calm dreaming still
Just smiling from time to time
That perhaps one day
Such dream can open me again
To go for, to wish, to feel you
Just as it was a moment ago?
So.. You have been inside me and where are you now, my darling?
Around still, with me, near?

Our sweet sin

It's a privilege
To stay
Your whore
I've never felt so good
Before
Licking
Smacking
Sucking
Oh, so sweet
Is our little sin
We grow up
Together in it
In to the new beginning
In to the life
We are
As we are
Poets
Lovers
Sinners
That's all because
You are so beautiful you
And you let me be
Your whore
You have a gift
To change the meanings
Of the words
My baby
My love
How it's sweet
Your cock
In my mouth
Let's start again
I wish to have you
In my hand now
We were there
In our small room
And we did
As we want
Yet still
So little me
You let me to show
To you
No time, no place
To use all charms
We have to meet again
But I'm afraid
We wont have the time to lose again
And I'll need just to taste you, feel you
Listen
And to be your girl
again
It's just suddenly I felt
Unsure a bit

Am I great enough
To be your love
This lady you need
Your queen
I can be your whore
Yes, this I can
I hope you were satisfied of me this way
Did my mouth work well for your pleasure,
Or should I learn more?
Tell me
I need to be your perfect whore
I need to give you the best love
I wish this and I want to know
How to give you more
And more
I forget to show you
My dance
We have to start again
This romance
You have to see me
Dancing for you
It's the part of the secret ritual
You have to see
I'm princess too
For you
But to be your whore
Was so good
You know
And I wish to be like this
Again
Yes, my man
I love to finger my self
Thinking that it's you
Doing it so sweetly
Still
I love you
Doing it
To me here
And in all of those places
Train, Cinema
Such a wonderful things
We create being together
I miss your smile
The way you move our steps
Harmoniously connected
Your arms on my waist
Holding me tight
Your hands in mine
Our kisses in the crowd
On a bus on a tube
And your face
Your eyes watching me now
My beautiful
Oh, how beautiful
You are.

Anarchy

How it is
That this little anarchy in love
Makes me so happy
I just worry a bit
How are you with this me
So open
Suddenly
Here

Discovering

With you
I feel like
I just discovered
How beautiful love and sex
Can be
With all this
What is
In this short space
Between my and your lips
or
other things
we use
to this

I love when you are good to me

I love the way you let me know
That you don't mind and that you love me what ever I do
And I won't lose you so easily as I'm always afraid that I could
You don't even know how much I love when you talk to me
How much I love that you are here still
I love when you are good and sweet
I love that you let me feel so good each time you come
However I'm able to express it to you
It's real and it's wonderful
My heart is yours
And this makes me feel
As never before
I learn each day to love you more
This is what I was born for

The scent

I wonder where
Do you feel the scent of me now
And how intense it is still in your mind
Can you see me still, can you find
In all of those places you were writing about?
Do you remember I asked you once
"Steal me"
You said that you already did
Really?
Wasn't just a loan?
I could think like this
When I don't see you now
Only your last words "don't worry"
Let me believe and let me be calm
I wish it could be forever.

We know the taste of paradise now

Picture of heaven
We created once
And we even touched this
Even tried
All of those tasty colours and smacks
All of those branches and fruits
We know, we tasted
Oh just why
I feel so moved
Watching some silly sexy movie
On one of those sites
And why I'm so sad
All this is so far away right now?
But you love you said
And you think every day
Of our time together
I have to wait then I know
It's just so hard sometimes
When there is no you around
Not even word any touch
Just a memory and promise
But I know you are here inside me still
And in all of those sites, places some faces too
And our words here and our souls
I feel so rich now though still hungry too
How amazing is this all with you right now.

Hungry poet

So hungry you are now
It seems like a picture
Of a man sitting on the branch
Who is watching His muse
And all scraps of her juicy cunt
Which is giving new light
To fulfill his mind
For more
Poetry
Is this good relationship to go on?
This little exchange of two mad minds
Dancing on the wall
Of our dreamlands?

The train

I had little dream about the train yes
Wasn't Orient Express?
And the stranger on the way
Whose glance makes me feel
So naturally naked again
And the journey was long
Very deep surprising, sweet...Yes
I love trains too I think so...

Tension

All is fine Yes
Just why each time it hurts the same
This lack of answer, this silence
I should used to this I know
I should be calm, happy and I am
Just this silence for a moment
Is so heavy still I can't stand this
But don't want pressure you too much
Do not want expect
You are perfect I know this so all that I can do
Is just to believe I know
It's just sometimes when I don't know what to do
To let you be close enough to listen your thoughts to hold
Be positive Yes I know it's all within my mind
It's not your fault I'm just too crazy now
I should fight with this tension inside
With such thoughts
It's an obsession not a love
But I love you Yes I do
I feel you in each little cell of me
You live inside here
So what all these worries about
I'm silly I know just be back soon my love.

Life with you

Life seems so exciting
When you have your lover beside still

Yes

Even this simple yes is more than enough to make my heart aroused

Muse

I know that my poetry
Makes you hard
Is this bad?

Don't say I won't find my home

What I can do with my wishing silly mind
Where to go with it
If I search nothing but love
But each time I'm closer to it
It seems I'm not able to drown deep
Is it something wrong with me?
What is this practical love you talk about
You don't believe I'm able to love like this?
You think I'm always far away from these who I should be with?
There is no help for me?
Please do not say this
I wish to hide right now right here
Not wandering anymore
There is no need
I know my heart and its greed
Don't say I want more than I should
Don't say I will never be able to find home
I'm a bit away now I know
My mind flies to another land
But do you think so
It will be always like this?
No I hope you are wrong
It was just another step to do
And right now there is another one
Finally I'll rest in his arms for good
Don't say I wont
You don't know this at all
Please don't say such words
I was never more sure anything but this
That one day I'll have to leave.

Somebody else is the lover

Maybe this can make you silent now
And I know it'd be lost
Not only for me but to the world
But this cunt
Which you crave for
Is closed

Library
She belongs to another race
Knowledge hunter
She follows good names
To use them
For her own progress

In mean time
We are here
Drinking
The wisdom
Of our shelves
Unwritten still
Books of emotions

The warrior

You are a big city warrior
And me just a water nymph
From one of these pretty looking lakes
You wish to go by one day
But you don't have the time enough
Busy in your big hard beautiful world
I'm waiting here still
Smiling because I know
That in fact you are here
Inside drowned quite deeply
Just as it should be
With me

When you say "I miss you"

When you say
I miss you
I just wish to get hold of your beautiful head
Put it tight to my breast
Kissing you on your sweet cheek
And kissing more
Your lips
Your eyes
Your ears
And go down too a bit
Just to see this wonderful rush desire in your glance
With such a great passion and love within
And all your trills and words
To feel and hear
I wish

Two birds

There is a beauty
In your words
That I can't deny
There is a spirit I love to drink
Day and night
There is a mystery I wish to follow too
And there is a story we create both
So merrily
Floating here
Among the pages of our own
Realities
We live
We are nothing but birds
Searching wild but cozy nests
Among the trees
Of our dreams
Smiling

Instead of all

Instead of all I loved when you say
That you respect my pussy
So you can't just come and go
And you will fuck it one hour or more
That was cute
Just as your cock
So different you are
From all
Even this wild part of you
Is just exciting and so good
This bad boy in you
Is wonderful
My sweet tender brutal you are
And this way it's a real pleasure
To be your whore
Yes, my love
You have a key to this door
Fits perfectly
Welcome

Any words

Any song in me today
Any dance, wish or play
Any word
Just this silent lack of you
Inside
Just this
I MISS YOU
I find

Silent

But after all
I'm happy to know
That I have the man
To whom I can tell
These words
Directly
And to feel even this
Silent answer in me
He is there He needs
And he feels the same
Just sometimes
Has no words as well
To tell how much
He misses me
So he is silent
Even more than me

I miss you

Each time you are silent for few days
What to do with my self
Yes some messages around me all the time
Yes some smiles poems comments
Yes all the world around
I still have
But when you are silent
For a few days
I'm so terribly heavy
And I can't think of anything else but this
That you are silent
Any message today again
I just wait to smile
I'm so addicted to your thoughts in me
I shouldn't maybe
Have to fight with this
Have to live
As before
Yes I know
But I miss you
I dream of you
Each night
I have you inside all the time
Can't wait to touch you again
And it's a madness I know
This love shouldn't be like this
I should breathe
Just simply doing my things
And waiting for new
Sweet dreams you bring
With you smile,
With your words,
With your spirit
With your love
I know
But I miss you!
And only this
I can feel
Still
When you are silent
So completely
Just few words I need
To breathe to live
You know this
Come back
To me
My darling

The parts of yours, which I love the most

I love your tongue and fingers the most I think
Oh and your voice
When you are saying all these sweet sexy things to me
Yes I love it
Of course I love your cock too
It's a really cute one
It's just that your tongue and fingers
Oh and this gorgeous voice of yours
Were first
So I love them
The most I think
Though yes it's hard to choose
What part of you is the sweetest one
I know
But this tongue penetrating me oh
And these fingers of yours
And the way you play with me by them
Oh and then all that you say
And your look
God how I miss this all
Right now...

Can't help

You are so good in this art of seduction
That's why I love you so much too
You were born to be my love
And to make me the most happy girl
Of this world You know?
Such a sexy guy as you
Makes me feel just wonderful
I can't help this why so?
I just want to sing this song for you
And follow you whenever you say I should go
And do whatever you ask for
That's why I was also born to, my love

Whenever

Whenever I go to you or you to me
I promise and
I always wish to keep
My legs wide open for you
Then bend over to show you my ass
Just ready
To make you feel this base primal need
To fuck me deep
Yes my man, I love it!

Yes do it please

I have a need inside me
I wish you to watch my hole
From behind
And touch it by your finger
Carefully
Letting it flow with fresh juices to taste
And then I wish you to smack it
Yes lick your finger now and put it again
Yes
I need you to watch me there
With your eyes open wide and your horny smile
I'm your bitch right now!
And I need you so much
I need you to be hard
Do not stop playing , please
Push it deeper
Oh yes!
And say that I'm your whore!
Yes I'm!
My love, please come inside, now
I want to feel your cock, wow
Yes
Oh yes!
My love!
My man!
Yes
Fuck me like this
Yes
Baby!
Please!

For you I am

I love the way I'm for you
Oh so free it is, so natural
I love as I'm right now
Just can't stand a thought
That you could leave
Or think bad of me
Then all this starts
Darkness among the stars
I try to reach all the time
In your mind in your heart
I drawn there and I go from years
So, please don't be afraid
To not have me for you only

My treasure

My treasure
You
This one
Whom I'm afraid to lose
Each day
I know I shouldn't
Come what may
I'll just keep my place
In your heart
I know that

Not all in one time

I love in you even this
That you show me your self
Piece by piece
You never hurry up with all
Except these moments
When we are together
As one

That train

I wish to be in that train
Which takes us to our room again
To feel this heat and longing in my veins
To hide my self in your arms, palms, mouth
And drown drown drown

Unspoken beautiful words

I love all these never unspoken billion words
That you wish to share with me but you do not,
I know that all of them are beautiful and special and cute
I remember how sweet are your thoughts and voice
I can create another billion sweet conversations between us
and never say any word so beautiful as yours
And this that stays between these lines
which we were able to share sometimes

Poet
I know the man
Who is ready to eat your body deeply
Just to write another piece of poetry
About the special taste of this
That he found inside it
Be Aware Poets are everywhere

Belt!

what ever your answer is
it always puts a smile on my face
I call it love
and I'm grateful
but are you sure?
belt not rope?
my love?

Days here

feed and happy
is there anything more I can say?
waiting, walking, eating, sucking, smiling, screaming, whispering, fucking, loving
the city is wonderful
what station are we at now, forget the name again

Wolfie lover

My wolf came into the forest
To take me
It's not the first time
Not the last one, he does so
Maybe because I love this
Quite inconspicuous smile
He has just between one and another
Feast of him by me

My sunny

You are still able
To make me
so happy
By a single word
My beautiful

Your call

You let me do bad things my beloved
I know you enjoy these sweet little crimes
Which flow from your to my soul
To link us together for good in the secret
We can't share with anyone
Flair mind you are
And I can't say no when I love
So we go together low
Right now

Are you still hungry?

Yes you can do it with a passion
Your special inner charm beautifully and strong
With all this that you can give so naturally to me
But if there is no real care for today for us
You know it seems a bit sad after all
And I become calm wishing less
I just wait now, I learn to live separately
For months, for years maybe
Is this patience good for this love?
Can passion survive in hibernation?
Well we will see my beloved
Are you still hungry as you were before?

Lookout

You answer my inner questions
Like you are living inside me
You know the best I need
You are waiting on your golden branch
Keeping lookout on me still
Touching dreams, this mad atmosphere between
Alluring, inspiring, sweet I like you here

Drifting

Yes I love all these sweet little stops
Swimming in your mind creations
When I imagine myself as this mermaid
Who sings for you another song
Leading you to a secret death
That you could drown once again
In this irresistible charm
Of immortal belief that we can wake up again
Just to dream to get lost one more time
The circle of our needs never ends
So we are here again and again
Having hope for more
That is how it goes that is how I love you here

This never-ending story

Hey you - the Lover
I know you exist for me only when you feel that I need this
So don't think I forget about you now
I just know that we have the time still
So I wait and play here
You know how I love this world
My waiting room
Is still full of dreams about you

Question

There is silence
On your site
When I don't write
Why?

Traveling in your mind

You seem angry a bit
Being now a piece of this dream
Used in a bad way perhaps
Waiting still for scraps to serve back
Your wonderful mind created for my pleasure right now
Yes I love to live here inside you
And mix you and him
Do what you want now I'm not afraid
I enjoy your part and I'm glad to find you

My own wolf

I wonder where is my wolf now
Is he hunting still so busy with a new dream to gain?
Or with all these things around him?
To arrange, to catch, to keep?
I love to imagine his life still
Even if it is so closed to me here
I do not belong to this forest he own I know
So I do what I want in my own world
He will come again one day
Wolves like to be free but this one still belongs to me
It's so sweet when I am sure
Time, place, words doesn't matter anymore
When we know what we know right now.

Who you are

You are just the right home for my thoughts to explode
You are the mirror I can see the right pictures of my own dreams
So you mix living here being the part
Of my own way through the light
Is it bad for you, is it hard?

No reason

It's just our writing that we share
We both long for their fingertips
(maybe you long for something else more)
So, wandering among sweet dreams or last pleasures
We meet here suddenly - two souls in need
Which understand each other perfectly
Just to spend some time here
No names, no faith
Simple thoughts to check
And to send something back
No reason for this but wish, a little spark among the dark
or among all other sweet things we live with
It is good to be here with you and your writing too

Your loving fingers

They know so much
They know how to touch
They know how to push
They know how to rub
They know how to slip
They know how to keep
They know how to wander here and there
They know where to press
They know how to undress
They know how to caress
They know how to arouse me
They know how to make me scream
They know how to make me wet
They know how to make me wait
They know how to make me sweat
They know how to make me hungry too
They know how to make me asking more
They even know how to make me begging you to stop
They know how to make me dream on and on
They know how to make me soft
They know how to make me
The woman in love
They even know how to hurt me
Beautifully
Indeed
Loving fingers they are
Admired

Some

Some people we feel inside
No matter where they are
It's a miracle of life
It's what matters
And what you really have

Easy going

We do not complicate things
We just have a little bit more
Than we had before
I didn't know it's so easy
until we met
but now
I just smile
and wait
for the next
step

At least

Even missing you badly at times
I feel good
When I know
That you are with me still
At least
Within your dreams

Colour

I'm not that noisy
As I used to be
You should know though
I still love you
As I did before
I just like this silence now
somehow

You who wait for words

I know you are waiting
But I have others
To feed up at the moment

For now

I love when you are there
Missing me
Leaving your sweet little traces
In our spaces
Then I know
That this journey through the moon
Will be continued
And don't say sorry
That you came
too late
You are always welcome
Even when I'm away
Just be
near
connected to my soul
as always
as you were before
It's enough
for now

Almost without you

Daily sadness and joys
Captured my soul suddenly
It's almost like you were not here
Anymore
Just sometimes this scream inside
Come back, come back
I really need you to live beside me
I need this hope
For more to go on
What ever I have to do right now
Right here
To live day by day
To not die inside
Without this special you
This dream too
This love

Until

Sometimes I can feel like your heart stopped beating
When I keep silence and the distance is killing this dream
But when I'm back and think of you more
I can see there is still you here for me
I love to come back to you
I love it and I will
Until you let me be near
Until I can feel
You want me still

Still
You are the last person I talk to
Yet still the closest one
My beloved

It's love which is perfect not we

Do we have to be perfect to love?
Always true to each other always good?
I don't think so it's love which is perfect for us
To catch each moment that comes each smile, longing, desire
Is love possible to get for good?
I don't know this yet
Instead I know how it is to have it inside
And smile with it and cry and live and fly
And go on, break sometimes too or lost or love more than one
It's so floating sometimes
Yes but some stay for good at least inside our soul
I call it the miracle I call it sweet love
I hide it or I show depends, the time is always a part of it
And me and dreams too and memories of course
And life goes on from one to another corner
From one to another love
The circle again, the way to follow
We never know we will stay or we have to go
We can come back too, I am sure
All depends of the flow and us and what we want
And how we can see each other as always the same, I know...
But it's how it goes with me and you
Let's fly let's love
Whatever it is it doesn't matter at all
No definitions we need to enjoy what we can have in this world.

Yes I am yours

Men sometimes like to give themselves to me
They write down on the letters they send "I am yours"
I never send them back the same
And they know I am just a bird they can't catch
And they let me fly but I always come back
To the nest of your heart
And I love to hear your words "You are mine"
Yes I am and I love to be your woman

You were here

So you were here again
With your hunger for more words
From me or other fluids so sweet
I like when our worlds mix
I like to be in your dreams
or wishes too
They are fine delicious and wild as you

Neurotic

I am still afraid there is too much of me here
And my words can touch you too much
Or that there is not enough love I show to you
And you can go away or that you simply can't stand
all this what I make around or that you stop believe
in you and me together
Why so full of fears is still between you and me
I can't explain

Truth

I am never untrue
In my heart or words of love to you
Maybe sometimes I just hide
One lover or few
To not upset you
That's all

Next time

Next time when we meet
Don't say any word just take me
The way you do so
Wild hard strong and free
I need this my darling so please do this to me

Don't stop

It's adventure time you said to me
And you are right and you know me well enough
To set me free right here
I love when you know what to do
To make me yours for good
And to let me love you more
You are only one man on this world
Who keeps me mad in love with you for years
It's so good You know?
It's so good don't stop

Layers

Some just can't see more layers we all wear
so they see only this what can be seen
all the rest is disgusting and insane for them
be careful for people with walls in their heads
they won't understand
they will be first to judge you and to let you down
better to leave a fight doesn't have any sense
they have to discover their own boundaries themselves
you have nothing to do there they won't understand
they are not ready yet and you can only fail
you this open one and insane beautiful loser
But in their eyes even not beautiful just mad
So free you are in your own mind
stay like this it's just another level of understanding of yourself
stay on your way to heaven or to hell
you know that all is just a journey
and you can leave or you can stay for a while
depends on you and your will
you are the creator of your destiny and your dreams
you are here the one who lives your life
don't stop then and go on your way
it's nothing you can do more just go
you know what you feel the best
and you know what is right and what is wrong in your case
you don't need poor advice from people who don't know
your mind and your soul they are not special to you at all.

We did this darling

you see baby
at least
some of our dreams came true
we did things
that we do not wish to make with others
they are precious
and only for us
marvelous

Little important details of your personality and acts

. Mostly these are
very little things
Which makes you so great
In my eyes
At least

Our fantasy

Is that true darling
Is it just that we want what we cannot have?
So why do I already feel you in me
you with me here?
I know it's a bit like a fantasy or dream
but it's still
you and me in this

My sweet addition

Is it anything I need more than this writing to you my beloved?
Any alcohol, drug or even sex can't replace the real delight
Of my connection here mind to mind
I just have a little hope that you read me
And it's good for your ear
To hear my thoughts to stay here
So bared I am with them
So confusing or repeating sometimes
They will be never so beautiful
As all sweet signs of your presence
Beside me
But I need them to live
and to feel you here

I don't need perfect lover

It's not a point to be so perfect lover at all
It's a bit more complicated
I am afraid
But how come you know it
It's the hidden part of the story

I know why we went so far

I can explain you why we went so far
Because we both like
Dancing on the thin line
Between heaven and hell
Inside our mind
That's why darling
But it's so good we know when to stop
Or rather you
Are this one who knows
But sometimes we have to
Try all what leads us to know more
About each other
Besides we had some fun with this
Don't you think?

You hit me sweetly

I am still watching
You
Wolfie boy
With this sex behind your teeth
And your golden words
Hidden in your swollen mouth
Always ready to hit
You look good
To me

He is listening

You talk like lovers do
You fill this gape
I hold on among the space
When my man is silent
Listening behind the doors
If I still make love
I am just reading you
It's almost the same though
Just more quiet
I devour you
In peace
Secretly

Let's go on

Don't be angry beautiful
We all have our own story to tell
Just sometimes we stop
To look, to give, to take
Or just to enjoy each others company
The way is long
There is so many days to fulfill
Still
We can even go hand in hand
Some time
Or you can have me
The way you wish
Especially in your dreams
This is free zone and I do enjoy
Your visions
Mr. Wolf

The centre

Where is the centre?
Here
It's you
Yes you
You are the centre
And all the action is around
Or in you
And you are on the way
From understanding to creation
Of your own life
It's nothing wrong to be in love a bit
I think
Or showing this or that
To someone you like
If you enjoy it

To Narcissus

I like you little Narcissus
You are as shy as me
We play here as two children
Using words
Like others use their hands and eyes
Or the rest of things they have

Me and Island

I think I like this Desert Island I chose to live in
With few eyes which keep watching my dreams
And this one heart I love to believe in and cherish here
Yes and these few minds and spirits I love to feel near me
I am used to this through years and I am not sure
There is something else I could enjoy more
Oh maybe just your touch again and your voice
and your smile of course
But it's still just the Island I live in
and It's you who came nothing else

Awareness

Growing up
Is just to put off another barrier you had inside as a child
To free away your soul from each rule
That others give to control your moves
Through the world
The more free you are inside
Then more of your steps are made by your own will
And more enjoyable they are and more clear
And you can smile more aware
Because you know that you can do whatever you want from now

He and you

I am sorry to say so
But you are nothing but a jealous man
With spirit not big enough
To believe in this love
And in human as well
You believe in your god instead
And it's good for you
But you are not bad enough
To understand my soul so good
As he do

Me and poet

You seem to be cruel and honest enough
To get my attention and respect

My demented dark attraction

You seem to know well what attracts a woman as me
I wonder where and how we can follow each other here
Yes you are special to me and I do enjoy your die-hard mind
I feel comfortable and familiar within its horny sight
I'll read you more
If you let me do so
It's delicious thing to eat and to live for

Fellows in a dream land

Some of us have very special dreams
Like you and me
Here
and there

Delightful

There is no other Power
I can believe any more
Except
This sweet one hidden
In your lips and palms
Leading me
To the real pleasure
And forgiveness

The Birth

From the first day
I came to this world
I know
What I am living for

It's how we've found each other

In this ocean
Of differences
It's so good
To find
Another Island
Of similarity

Yang Ing

It's so good
To find each other
Now we can build
Our heaven and hell
Our castle and immortality
On the island of our dreams and reality

Did you come to save me?

Nice to see you again
Wolf man
I know you're just passing on
My desert land
But we both know
There are some dreams
That we could give
To each other
We can smell them
In the sight
Of our footsteps

The reason

I need to be with you
Because
You are the one
I am able to fly with
And flying
Is the one thing
I really enjoy
In this world

Humans

Yes men are not perfect
And we can lose them suddenly
That's why they are so beautiful
And we have to enjoy each special moment
That comes with them and goes too

Touches

The right touch
And I show you how much love is inside me
How deep you can go and it seems there is no end to it
The wrong touch
And I am not here anymore

Nothing else...

There is nothing else I wish to be
Than the beauty you have in your dreams
And you long for in the morning

It is still for me

I am here
For all those never written poems
I can feel in the memory
Of your kisses
I wonder how many lives
I can have at the same time
Still being myself in this
It seems that at least two
Just as we are
Right now

Exception

I hate anyone who tells me what to do except you
You are cute even in this and I am glad to listen - You
It's always the part of this sweet game we play
Even not being aware to the end
We create another day in our play
Where could I find something more beautiful?
Where could I drown so blissful?
I don't know
I never found
Anything more exceptional
So far

Power

I love to give you power
Over my body and soul
Because I love you and I trust you enough
To know that
You won't use it
In any other way
Than to make me smile even more
At the end and more open for you
As I ever thought that I could
It's the most wonderful thing
I ever felt
and it's good

Love is for these who are able to survive

We are so easy to touch
This jealousy of love is impossible
It lets only the strongest one survive
All the rest have to leave this boat
Before they do something wrong
or drown too deep to still live and sing
Her song

A future

Future
It doesn't matter
When right now right here
I feel eternity
In this little message
You keep to send still
and heaven is in me

Romance

I like the fact
That you are not afraid of death
If it comes
From my hand

Distant lover

You always just let me be
Hungry for you more and it works
All I have so far
Is this desire for more you
Inside my world and my hole

Wrong steps

I do all that I shouldn't do
Looking for general laws or directions
but I still feel your breath
beside me
maybe it's just a dream
but sweet still
so I keep
drifting in thoughts
into your world
opening my secrets to you with this hope
that it's not too much for you
and you rather stay silent
than you say go
because you can't stand me anymore

You must believe you hold a key

You are the one I gave the key
Into my world
I hope you do not destroy
What you hold

I am not sure
I'd be able to enjoy it still
If I don't have you
You who can do whatever
You want

How I wish you could be excited at least
Once or two
Or in tears or in smiles
Just looking at me
From inside my dreams
And sins

It should be amusing
A bit at least I think...

A request

Just tell me
When you stop your love for me
So I know the date
of my death

In meantime

Love

I learn still how to please you
Reading books of all possible kinds of behaviors people do
Bad or good doesn't matter my love
I just wish to be a good whore
In moments we are together
·   All the rest of the time
I have fun or wait or love
I know it's hard sometimes to handle
But I try
Why?
To keep my self happy free and wild
Just as I love and you love me to be
I think
or to make you a bit mad
well I am also bad
Just as you like

Writers and lovers

With writers and poets
As with lovers
Sometimes it's better
To try them all
Before you decide which one
Fits to you the most

Ps My dear poet friend
I am sorry I read another one more
But you know I'll be back to you soon
So do not worry and write still
If not for me so for them

Slight difference

Strange thing
Sometimes I can't find big difference between
Poets I read here
And lovers I give myself to
I feel the same unfaithful
When I stop with one to start with another

How I love to have my heart open wide for you
Now you can fuck my mind
Even more than you could do this
With my cunt

Proportions

In each life
There is time of passion
As there is time of boredom
There is place for love and hate
There is time for work and rest
And so on

Just proportions
Make some differences
I suppose

Summer wine

Another summer ahead
lets drink some wine
Instead
of other things
we could do
If we were able to move

Flowers instead how nice

Oh I didn't know
You killed your wife
Some time ago
It is so kind of you
To bring flowers on her grave
And give her prayer or two
So she rests now
and smiles to you
You are good boy today
What a nice surprise for her
Do you think she cares?

At least

So you insist
To not let me be so sure
Of you still
Good that at least
At the end
Of my despair
You come to say
This
What I need to hear

To live

Walking shadow

You
A bottomless pit
Where I drink my water
Of dreams
To feed myself
The way I wish

Your silence
Is the most courageous food
For my craves
I still hide before
Blind eyes
Of the crowd

As your words
Are balsam
For all longings
You put me in

To let me want you
More
And to let me
Drift on my way
With more passion

With the little help
Of your assurance

That we belong
To each other
At the end

Imagination

I love to imagine myself
That it is you
Who still look at me
here

Commandment of love

"And you won't have any gods before me"

I am your goodness
And you are my lord
From now on we can enjoy the world
As it is written in the old book of love

Too much between

But you know
Between you and me
There is still so much of all these things...
That sometimes I just dream
Of simple smiles
And a simple kiss
And that it could
Take longer than these few moments
In space we can have

Some special intimate things

These are things in this world
Which remain beautiful
As long as they are intimate
Between two... let's say few
Just make them public
And they lost their charm
Forever

Moments of truth

At times you feel like you are a bit lost
In all these dreams that lead you through this life
Yet I hope that in the right time you know
This perfect choice
Just when you really feel it
And when you know what you want

Do not spoil these moments of truth
They are really rare
And they are good

Vanity Fair

There is a lot of colours in life to enjoy
In each time you have something to discover and go for
Yet this one is still the most precious for all
No matter where it is found and for how long
Happy are these who know its taste
Unhappy too because anything else
Can't be enough when it is lost yet life has still its charms and joys
Of course
Of course

The Gypsy's wife

I just need to go now
To dance and to know
The taste and the smell of this life a little bit more
After all I'll be back
I'll knock on your door
As before
Asking for love
Like a dog

And you will let me come
Because it all was written in this book
We live in

And you accept this
Because you know me enough
To let me dance
Still
I'll be back to you
Or I'll die

Doesn't matter
I had you

So everything now
Is just a bonus
To enjoy

But l did all what I had to do
With you
I did good
All that I could

To feel you

So I go now
To enter the life

More wide

Good bye
For now

Our little play

And see darling
What we have done
A womanizer
Dirty boy
and your naughty bitch and whore

What a beautiful couple

I will miss us now

Who can play the same
As you and me?
And to keep this so innocent still?
Just like a dream
Of perfect love

We had once and we had to lose
Oh you were here too
For sure
At least for some time
My partner in crime

But we went too far
I know
Though
It was worth it

Licking wounds

Love is at times as a war
We are licking our wounds right now
Soon another battle can come
Who knows?
Just as in a war
We can expect everything
And we have to go for it
Because we need this

So I stay here
As before
On the scene
Of my private show
For one actor mostly
Sometimes more

Where shall I go?

Lost again

The city is calling
Nights still open before
And you strangers
Sing your songs

Like you know
What I want

Of course I am lying

And who will lie to me
So sweetly as you did?
I'll wait for a man like you
Or I'll dream and learn how to lie too
To let them feel good

What else I can do?

Next level

With some of you
I don't need to talk any more
We know enough
Now I just wish you
To do it

We don't need more
Just this

One of the important questions

Are you still curious of me?

How to stay young

You just count the time
From one to another event
That matters to you
Everything between
Does not exist
So you saved some of it

A thousand years

The time was never important
For us
And never will be
We are above this
In our dream of eternal love
That can't be crashed
By any little thing
Of our humble existence or weakness
In just one of all possible worlds
We chose to stay for a while

Immortal beloved

I wish to die in your arms
Can you promise me this
My sweet?

Hard to say

Did I break your heart again
For good perhaps
Or did I make you laugh?

I hope this second more

Yet you have been gone
So I am not sure how bad I am for you

Gypsy's wife

My dear man
I wonder if one day
After another age flows
You just stand on the scene
To sing the song for me
I'll be back hearing your voice
I'll be back of course
Because
Each way has its beginning
and the end we both see the one
You and I in song
Remember?
So I'll be back hearing your voice
I'll be back of course

Groovy kind of love

I love when you said last time:

"You don't have to be polite Anna
I love you"
You know that either you...
And you are not
We are just as we are
You hidden at times
Me open wide

Each has its ups and downs
I know honey I know
This even too much
At times

But it is fine
It is this mystery on the way that leads us
This is all the fun in it
Isn't it?

Oh darling it all seems ok as long as I feel love in the air
But what if this all disappears one day?

What will stay?
The memory of glorious ancient times

So is it worth it, does it have value
Yes, yes

To jump now
Into the life
Just as we can just as we want
and smile and cry feeling all this again and again
Because there is still nothing else

Worth a while more
I suppose...

Except one thing...

But you are not here

Love...

Is sometimes a simple joy from little signs I can see
And faith that you still live there for me

To one of wolves

Sometimes when you come here
I see
You just check if this is the right moment for you
And after few words you know

It is not
yet

So you go away
To check again
After year
Your meal

This little book to fulfill

I wonder if this is what I do
Makes you feel more horny
Or rather sick though

But I don't care
It's just my way to go
You have nothing to do with this
For now

Even if you still live
here

Somehow

I know it seems that I am a bit cruel for you
Maybe it's just because

You already know
all

Empty spaces

So it was me
Who killed this love
Finally
Now it's time for a little dance
In the dark
And for this feeling of being invisible again
Yes it was best like this
After death there will be another life instead

Just as you said

Coming back to life

Indeed at the end
There is always you
Who know yourself the best
So only you can understand why
Some actions were done
Some promises broken
Some feelings killed

Yes it is you who know all the story
Of your bright and dark soul
It is you
Who has to fight every day
With your own games
and try to win at the end
another day

With a little bit of spice in it
To enjoy its taste
The best

The variety

In fact there are only a few things that matter in life
And from now all depends on how you can see and feel them
How you are able to describe, talk, live by it

There are only a few things
But such a huge variety in the way we get them
Indeed there is nothing more - just this
And time to understand or spoil things

It's about

It's not all about just taking and giving
It is about a feeling of primary joy and openness
It is all about being free and safe
On the way to each other on the way to an adventure
That the future of both of you seems to be every day
Like it was still just the beginning

Little smile to my own world

It's so easy to be the Queen
In my home made
United Kingdom

Gone but still inside me

Do you think it is the end when you have gone ?
You are wrong
I can now even feel you more
You became my every thought
Dream and joy
You became sweet memory of my own
Bitter too
I know you like to be like this
It's more tasty, more real
I know you my broad minded and down to earth man
And now even when you had to go away
I still own you like a dream I wish to stay forever in
I know how to keep you still
And I don't ever wish to cure myself
It'd be like a cutting half of me
This more beautiful, more mad and deep
I won't do this
I'll drown with this ship
Instead

Dance me to the end of love

I am always the same
And I back to places I love the most
It's just how it is
And how it should be
The way is always the same
As you know well
We don't need to hurry up
to the end
We can dance still
Or I can
Your choice
I'm here

Always inside my own madness and dream
I'm not going anywhere

So you can do
If you enjoy

Come and dance me
To the end of love

A perfect man for me

It has to be a boy still
Naughty, free
But always good and gentle for me
Even being harsh at times when it's needed or sexy... depends
But he knows when he can
The man who never pushes me to do things I'd not wish to do my self first
But who let me wish all these things to do...

Yes perfect man
Who is you
It's good to meet
At last

and keep or lost
Doesn't really matter
It's just a matter of time and place and life as you can say
But this what you have because of him
Stay forever
In your soul
Like a crack like a goal
Just to keep just to dream about
And dance inside your soul
Just like this to go on

Sweet temptation

Another sweet temptation
Is growing inside my world
It's you my wolf

You delightful man
Who comes to me
Each time I call my love
Dancing on my burning fields
After another war
We just had a moment ago

You who support me when I am weak and alone
You who watch my dance when I got strong
You who could be my love
As well
Yet for now
My soul-mate
I adore your presence here
You know
And I appreciate
This hope
For more

Just watching you still

I think there is nothing but poetry
In your life
But this is a main reason I love to come back to you
and watch
Even not touching you
Nor saying a word
Even not being your woman, love or whore

I am just coming here
and drink your mind
Like it was my story and like you were mine

Nothing new

You just compare:
Sensitivity
Believes
Dreams
Chemistry

Then you go for it

You feel this mixture of smiles and tears
And you know
That's it

Nothing new
Indeed

Yet so sweet

A thing about treasures

I like to find my treasures by myself
When someone try to push me
To buy them
I don't like them anymore

The beautiful thing for me has to be find by me
Then it pleases
And it is special and sweet

Golden words

Two Gold maxima of our love:
"I don't trust you because I know you"

And whatever we do together and no matter how far we go through this you can always say:
"I haven't done anything that you didn't ask for"

And it's true you perfectly know me and this that I want you to do to me
You perfectly know how to make me feel good being beside you
That's why I want you

Love and death

You are only one man who's hand I could die from and still keep smiling
Love is so close to death

You can feel happy to die when it is needed
as you can feel death in you when it is gone
This love

Amazing it is
And so full of surprises

There is still something to live for
and enjoy
Like your breath inside my mouth and the taste of your tongue
or the way you touch me telling me what you want to do to me
and how gentle you are with this and brutal too
Just amazing how you make me feel so good, so yours

I have never met anything anyone more delicious on my way
Than you

So far...

About a death and hope

Death - just the end of this play
But don't worry if your faith is strong
And you are good you have a chance
To go to the second level

Some nights I can feel you there

Some nights I can feel you are there wolf
I am just not ready yet
To come

My head is too busy
and my thoughts still belong to another man

Yet each time we meet
I am happy you are here
Waiting and leaving your footprints
In my longing town

One day our time can come
For now only these few smiles that we always feel
Can save us close to each other

I know you want more
That's why I can't come
Yet

Our little silent talking game

Yes I enjoy to listen your silence
Just forgive me if sometimes
I can be wrong with interpretation

You know it's everything about the feeling and imagination
And this can leads to unknown or to being a fool!
Even in such a familiar topic
As my own and your soul
In this little play
We go on
Somehow

Waiting still

This what you gave me
Is all this free space
For dreams

and from this time
All depends from how deep and wide
I can jump, swim, see and feel
Whatever I wish

And you are somewhere here
Waiting still

Behave as you came first here

Yes making mistakes is a human thing
The point is to know or to learn
When and how
Turn around

To stay on your way
This right one
With enjoyment and song and dance
Inside

Just to make few more footprints
In this book of life
Making it more precious more wide or funny too
Before we leave
For good

The story of life

Well in fact
it's nothing but the story of meetings, leavings and their
consequences

Evolution

Life is an evolution
But you missed my direction
So it seems I go alone
In to the unknown

It's not a point

In love
There is not a point
To be always so perfectly honest and true
To each other
More it's to feel comfortable being as you are
And still feel safe that whatever it can be
All will be fine
And you are still the right one
And dear for him
And the same from another side

Of course
That's how it works

About love again

Yes it must be true
Love is just a magical, fragile, intimate
experience of your own soul
It's good if you have possibility to express this somehow
To share with this one
Yet you must be careful
Too much love can be hard to stand
I suppose
So just dance in your heart
And learn how to not scare away
This someone you care
This delicate sound is the best to gain
Not too loud not too much
Just dance inside first
Enjoy or suffer and play within
With this feeling that comes so rare so sweet
Sometimes stay silent too
If it works good

It is a fragile thing
This love
More waiting in this than fight
It comes naturally
In sounds, touches and kind of wisdom

Don't make too much noise
Just listen its voice
And never use force
Rather a beautiful song
To let her know
That you love

No words needed

Somehow words don't flow anymore
It seems like I've said everything to you
There is no need for more
Repeating could destroy
The meaning
of us

So now only a play of thoughts
Inside my head
Let me dance
Still for you

So I do

My Grand book of wishes

First of all
I wish you to follow my thoughts
Even these silly, boring, repeating ones
With these all errors I do
And that you try to understand them all
I know it is all mad at times
Touching too and it makes you feel
Bad or good
But you have to look

You have to look at me
Without it it's nothing here

And love is just the word
Without the real background

And I wish it was true
This all you
Not only the moment in space
For naive silly whore
Who is looking for something
She should not
No this I don't want

I wish a few things more
But this I wrote before
So you know
And I wish this one night too
With you
And that you massage my feet
Being again so caring and sweet
Telling me all I want and need to hear
Making me yours for good
Yes this I wish the most
And that all you say was true
And that I was able to catch this somehow
and never lose
And I wish to be more sure
Of tomorrow
With you

I know it is too much...

We become a bit cruel with time

We are getting to be a bit cruel
With time
Have you noticed?

Keeping these little sorrows
Years by years
We do not even know
When it starts

You have to be ready
To face this now

On this stage of life
We are

After all we went through
Together
You should be aware

What I can do to you
When I feel not enough

Love

Sinners and honest men

Sinners and honest men
Will never understand each other

So better if the stay away
And play different games

They are not friends

Aspiration

What is your favorite aspiration?

I'd like that someone find the hidden beauty
In me
Then make a piece of art from it
And invited me to the process
Of Creation
And... we could both just disappear
After all

About some wonderful things

You know what is wonderful between us Darling?
That whatever we do
Even being hard at times, bad, impossible, wrong
Or not being at all for long
Still whenever I see you
I can feel like this adventure just began
and it's so exciting and so good
To be near you
And this mix of smiles and tears inside
And this comfortable confidence
That I am beautiful for you
Yes it is sure
In your smiles it is
And in the way you kiss
I can't explain this well
But it's just
That anything else
Doesn't really matter and doesn't compare
And we can do or say whatever
It'd change nothing at all
Smiles and tears will go on

Silence and sounds

Sometimes it's like a sea of silence
You have to get through
Waiting for noises
You long to make
In the darkness
One more time

A way

Is any other journey for human worth a while
than this deep one in to your heart and mind?

We can travel just on the way to each other
and explore this as much as we can

Walking on the fields cities and deserts seems quite empty thing
If it doesn't let you know more about yourself and about someone else...

Sweet secrets

There is so delightful sweetness
In some hidden secrets
If you know how to keep them
Alive
And to feed yourself
By this violent kind of pleasure
You can taste in them
When they become
The most valuable and mysterious
Part of your life.

Then there is no return
From this deeper kind of world
You live by
Or you live because

Until death
or
Until they become
Ready to be shared
With all
But be aware
They can lose its natural charm
Or they can transform
To some new form

But do not hurry up with this
You never know
So
For now

Just enjoy
And keep them still
As deep as you need

They are
To make your days and your life

So SPECIAL

Art is everything

Anything you are not able to turn in art
Is nothing special

And it doesn't really matter what the word "art" means to you

It's everything
You can live for

Hidden sky

In the framework of your hidden love
I can feel freedom just enough to fly
And to share the flutter of my wings
With you

I don't need to go away
Because your chains
Are wide enough
Invisible but strong
So I know where I belong
And I wish to be back still
Yet I go my way discovering this world
Like a child
And we both know that this is what I need and I enjoy
So we have this large space and time to play
And this is ok
As long the memory of your sight
Is still alive

A question...

What form of me you wish to have now my dear?
How to love you still
When all seems so distant again
suddenly somehow
Far away

but always
I do and you too

so come whenever you need

my love

Me and write

What are you doing there at night?
I set free demons into the sky
So they can enjoy a little freedom
Are you all right?
Yes all fine

This mortal coil

If at times I do not play soft enough with you
Forgive me
It's because
I am always aching without the sight of you
No longer sure of anything
Then thoughts go mad
Playing their battles defending, hitting you
for my own uncertainty
I feel because you are no longer here

So little I have you
And so much I feel you I see you inside my head

It never change
See my darling, so many years and it's still like we just have met
And it was the beginning of the story
Each day each year the same
Yet so different
But today I learn one more time
How to take a pleasure from this silent signs
You give
To let me know you are here still
For me

The night is over

I'm so happy you came again
Lover
You recognize well
My call in the dark
Then you are
My wolf

Turning tears in to smiles
Just like that
By one snap
So easily you do that
and the night is over

The spy

Do you feel me
On the other side of this screen
So much as I feel you?
Whenever you come closer here and make a single step
I see it I am the spy in our house of love
I can't help I see all you do
I almost feel your breath and your thoughts
and I share I share as much as I can
until I feel you are so close
and dreams grow up fast in mind
and maybe you hear my thoughts for a while..
and you enjoy and I wish I wish
you could stay here for me longer a bit just a bit
until another dream I can share and I can live by
comes because you are here again for me so close

The tree of dreams

A hundred dreams
Come inside
Whenever you touch me
By your beautiful mind
Don't stop please

go on and stay here near

so I can feel them
and live enjoying their melody and smell
so easy to touch they are now

like you were here
beside
inside
me
still
I love it
and I always will

The best that you do

The best thing in this that you do
Is the way you make me feel beautiful enough
To wish to seduce you
and this is all I long for
to be like this to you

seductive and beautiful

Love and poems

I love that
Writing another poem for you
is a bit like making love
With the same man from years
and still with the same flame
it comes each day each night each year...

It's an art and love in one
So perfect bound so fine

and

I love that
I can still
Enjoy this one single favorite topic in me
I have it from the time we've met

At times I am just not sure
How much you enjoy
this open love

yes I know this writing on this site
Is like showing me naked one more time
before all who comes to watch us...

but you love a bit naughty things too
so you can enjoy I am sure you do

and I love that I can be mad with you as much as I want
It's quite comfortable

Bad boy

How bad I have to be today
To be exciting for you
My bad boy?

Hard to say all is born in a moment you come
But everybody knows

That being just nice
Is not enough

For this juicy colourful life we go through
to gain new smiles
together

Just a spark of your sight

So this is the end for now...
Not a day but maybe a month or a year
of waiting
I was too intense perhaps
So now it's time to calm down

You have gone
Nothing to share
Nothing to live by inside

Just a memory of the spark
and hope

that you will be back

I am not creative

No my darling man
I am not creative
I just need to tell my story
When something special begins
and it all starts with you
Each time you come
My beautiful open book
My adventure with no other end
Just with you
In your arms again
Cuddled

It's you this sweet raise the roof of my head
I love to have
To move, to scream, to wait
and to show
what I find so beautiful
in this life in this world...

Don't you know?

Tomorrow

It's amazing how easily you make me so hungry so greedy
and one day seems again like an ocean of longing
to have you again the way I need
just for me

In life

In life
there is time of fuck
and there is time
of poetry
less interested of this make wars
or other bad things
besides we are all just a voyeurs
of other people life and fantasies

of course in mean time there is plenty other things we do like hard work for living and some daily stuff
like making our beautiful children growing up if we have some, keeping family and friends in good or
bad mood, but it's nothing what I am talking about right now

this what I mean is us and basic forces that lead us to act

love and hate
and space between
one or another feeling that let us move
in this world

right or wrong

basic things but natural...

I don't know where this smile came from suddenly
in me...
must be again some sweet memory...

A balance

At times I am a bit confused
Of how much lies we need to spread around
To keep all close to us happy enough...

It's also an art to know this
balance between right and wrong weight of illusion...

House of love

With you
Even a grand serious LOVE with all its hard rules and consequences
Seems attractive and not scaring at all
and this lack of freedom at our home
you announce
Is like an open gate to the unknown world of wonders so wide
That I never felt outside
It's like enter to real story I was only read about
So far...

Empty house

There is not love here anymore
So don't come

If you ask

If you want to know what I like
Well I like fishing in the great depth of life
Catching sparks

My fresh breeze

I love the way you are for me
This fresh breeze in the air
You gonna make me smile
Each time I see you here
You make me feel
Young forever with you
A dancing girl
Just as I love to be
My dear boy
My dream
Go on please

I need to put a spell on you every day new

I have a spells in my head
Those need to spread
Like I want you to be mine forever
Like I need you to be here
In any form available
You can be a link in net
A sound of the song you send on your site
A message
A hope for a meeting
A trill of the sight of you
But you have to be near
With me always
Because I don't know if I could ever enjoy this world
Without you
So I will spread this song
To keep you with me
Just like this
In my dreams still
Until another day will come
A day for us and our love
in touch

Pain of love

This love seems painful at times yes
I didn't know though how much this beautiful pain I need
To live
Until we've met

Am I able to hurt you?

If the answer is YES
so you are the right one

The importance

Nothing is more important
Than this what can happen
Between us
If it isn't
It means
That nothing really happens
Don't you know?

The slight differences

I am trying to save this all
What you are trying to hide
From some point of view
I can see kind of cooperation between us
In this matter
I will save all this what you will lost
And you will save all other things around
Thank you

Needs

I need to be like an open book
You need to be a secret lover though

And we both respect each other
This way love turned into signs in space
And our minds create magic to live by
Just like a faith
And hope

It is somehow wonderful
And you know that magic is all I can believe in
Especially this one that we can feel

Hidden things and exceptions

Generally I don't like hidden things
At all
Except these few
That I share with you

The temperature of love

Too many words
Too much heart away
It was too much of me by your side today
So it's time to go away
Waiting

A Mistake

For a moment I thought
That it is a conversation
But it's again just a talk of mad woman in space
Nothing else
How sad

An alternative

If we can't live together
Maybe we could die together
At least?

The killers – Shadow play

The killer can be a woman who brings your child
The killer can be a man you spent the night with
The killer can be a life you can't bear

Be strong if you wish to stay to the end of the show
If not, well it's just a matter of time
But why worry so much
Enjoy and find this real thing you care about
It has to be something special for you
Another way, what would be worth this entire world?

The answer is always the same and you know it well
So why worry now?
Stay strong and smile to all
That's how it works

It must be love

You make me feel sick too easily
It must be love

Resignation

Now I don't need to hurt you nor do anything else
It's time to simply live like nothing happen
It's not a first time like this and well
There is really nothing to fight for

So

Let's move on

Little thing

When there is not much to gain
There is not much to lose as well
So you live your life as it was before
Just without

Smile, smile not

Yes you know how to put smile on my face
But you know as well this how to get it away
It's just that I take all too seriously
So it's touching

So silly I am
With this

But how not to be
When I feel
Each word of yours
By all senses
By whole heart
And soul
How?

Dear reader I hope you enjoyed this special edition of poetry this is collection written by heart we all have these moments in life that we wish stay longer here you could find them I hope you may find your self here as well and that we share common ups and downs in our secret feelings grounds

Anna Cellmer